1984

Work, for the Night Is Coming

Winner of the Walt Whitman Award for 1980

Sponsored by The Academy of American Poets, the Walt Whitman Award is given annually to the winner of an open competition among American poets who have not yet published their first books of poetry.

Judge for 1980: Galway Kinnell.

Work, for

JARED CARTER

the Night Is Coming

MACMILLAN PUBLISHING CO., INC.

NEW YORK

Macmillan Publishing Co., Inc.
866 Third Avenue, New York, N.Y.   10022
Collier Macmillan Canada, Ltd.

Library of Congress Cataloging in Publication Data

Carter, Jared.
    Work, for the night is coming.

    I. Title.
PS3553.A7812W6   1980   813'.54   80–26221
ISBN 0–02–522090–X

10   9   8   7   6   5   4   3   2   1

Printed in the United States of America

ACKNOWLEDGMENTS

Grateful acknowledgment is made to the editors and publishers of the following publications for permission to reprint the poems indicated: *Ascent*, "Gathering Fireflies," copyright © 1978 by Ascent Corporation; *Backcountry*, "At the Sign-Painter's," copyright © 1980 by Cheat Mountain Poets; Barnwood Press Cooperative's chapbook *Early Warning*, "Walking the Ties," copyright © 1979 by Jared Carter; *The Chowder Review*, "The Birdstone," copyright © 1978 by *The Chowder Review*; *Green's Magazine*, "Monument City," copyright © 1980 by Green's Educational Publications, Inc.; *The Indianapolis Journal*, "The Madhouse," copyright © 1976 by Community Development Communications, Inc.; *Indiana Writes*, "Watching by the Stream" and "Bridge over Yellow Cat," copyright © 1980 by the Trustees of Indiana University; *Kansas Quarterly*, "Landing the Bees," copyright © 1980 by *Kansas Quarterly*; *The Nation*, "Early Warning," copyright © 1979 by Jared Carter; *The Participant*, "Sam Bass," "Oliver P. Morton," and "John Dillinger," copyright © 1969 by Radical Publishing Company of Indiana, Inc.; *Pembroke Magazine*, "Mississinewa County Road," copyright © 1979 by *Pembroke Magazine*; *The Pikestaff Forum*, "The Undertaker," copyright © 1980 by Pikestaff Publications, Inc.; *Prairie Schooner*, "Geodes," copyright © 1978 by the University of Nebraska Press; *Pteranodon*, "For Jack Chatham," copyright © 1980 by Patricia Lieb/Carol Schott; *Published Poet Newsletter*, "Turning the Brick," copyright © 1980 by Quill Pen Publishing Company; *The South Dakota Review*, "Meditation," copyright © 1979 by the University of South Dakota; *Sou'wester*, "The Measuring" and "Weather Prophet," copyright © 1979 by the Board of Trustees of Southern Illinois University at Edwardsville; *WIND/Literary Journal*, "The Oddfellows' Waiting-Room at Glencove Cemetery" and "Roadside Marker," copyright © 1980 by Quentin R. Howard; *The Spoon River Quarterly*, "The Strawman," copyright © 1980 by David R. Pichaske; *Poetry*, "Ginseng" and "Shaking the Peonies," copyright © 1980 by the Modern Poetry Association. "Glacier" was first published in the *New Yorker*. The author thanks the Indiana Arts Commission for a Literature Fellowship which aided in the preparation of the manuscript of this book.

FOR *Robert* AND *Cleva Carter*

Contents

For the ultimate sign of our disbelief in our own souls is our inability to believe in the souls of anything else around us.

TESS GALLAGHER

ONE

Geodes

THEY are useless, there is nothing
To be done with them, no reason, only

The finding: letting myself down holding
To ironwood and the dry bristle of roots

Into the creekbed, into clear water shelved
Below the outcroppings, where crawdads spurt

Through silt; clawing them out of clay, scrubbing
Away the sand, setting them in a shaft of light

To dry. Sweat clings in the cliff's downdraft.
I take each one up like a safecracker listening

For the lapse within, the moment crystal turns
On crystal. It is all waiting there in darkness.

I want to know only that things gather themselves
With great patience, that they do this forever.

Early Warning

WHEN the weather turned
Crows settled about the house
Cawing daylong among the new leaves.
It would be a hard spring,
Folks said, the crows—
They know. There are folks
Up near where I come from
In Mississinewa County
Who study such things.
Folks who believe tornadoes
Are alive: that polluted streams
Rise from their beds
Like lepers, following after
Some great churning, twisting cloud.
With their own eyes
They've seen a cyclone stop,
Lap up electricity
From a substation, then make
A right-angle turn
And peel the roof off some
Prefabricated egg factory.
Thousands of hens, who've never seen
The light of the sun, or
Touched earth with their beaks,
Go up the funnel like souls to God.

Weather Prophet

FOUND, on the back stoop, frozen stiff
On the morning after the storm
Under a fingernail moon, this old
Keeper of bees, string-saver, knower
Of clouds; whom the neighbors consulted
Faithfully each autumn for news
Of approaching snows, who was said
To divine with wooly-worms on bark
And tell rain a week in advance.
Who carried instead like extra bones
A pound of shrapnel from a boche mine
That lit up like a parachute flare
At the slightest barometric change;
And who, having outlived the bees
And the last friend who could recall
That war, took down a jar of pear wine
And went outside in the snow to wait
For something to pick him up—
Hopefully horsedrawn. And slow.

The Madhouse

I CANNOT give you the squeak
Of the blue chalk on the cue tip,
The sound of the break, or the movement
About the table, like a ritual of wine;

Then I was not born. My father,
Who saw it, was still in high school;
And there are others who remember
The poolroom on the avenue.

Here lounged the former heroes
Of the high-school team, who took
The Tri-State Crown in '24, and tied
With Massillon in '25. Catholics all,

A backfield composed of Swede
Svendson at fullback, the Baxter brothers
At either half, and handsome Richard
O'Reilly at the quarter.

They had no peers, then or now.
On Saturdays regularly they stood,
Hats firmly on their heads, watching
The procession of hooded Klansmen

Coming up Anderson Street, heading
Toward the Main intersection. Always
The Klan demanded hats removed
Before the flag they carried,

Always the boys at the Madhouse refused,
And began unscrewing the weighted ends
Of their pool cues. People came to watch;
The police stood apart; the Klan

Never got past the Madhouse. That
Was years ago. They're all dead now,
Swede and the Baxter boys, and
Handsome Richard O'Reilly,

Who married the banker's daughter;
And the Klansmen too. Only the men
Who were boys then can still remember.
They talk about it, even now,

Sitting in Joe's barbershop
Watching cars go by, or sipping a beer
In Condon's tavern. It is a story
I heard when I was a boy. Lately

There's been a doughnut shop
Where the Madhouse used to stand.
Mornings when I stop for coffee
I can almost hear it: the nine ball

Dropping in the corner pocket,
The twelve rolling to within an inch
Of the side; voices in the street
Echoing along the store fronts.

For Jack Chatham

For Jack Chatham, and his brother Tom,
Both without helmets, their red hair
Streaming behind them in the wind;
For all those who rode big Harleys
And Indians back in the fifties,
Who dropped out of school, of work,
Of everything, to drive again and
Again down the dark cylinders of air.
For Jack on that bright day hitting
The slick on the bridge and landing
Exactly in the center of Fall Creek
So that coroners from adjoining counties
Argued over his body while the deputies
Took Tom down the road to a place
Where the Klan hung out and bought him
A few beers and patted him on the ass
Saying it's all right, kid—
Go on riding while you got the chance.

Walking the Ties

THIS was the old woman who ate canned dog food
This the red wagon she pulled through the alleys
This the pack of stray dogs that went with her

Here are the boys who shouted and threw things
Here are the barrels of trash they all searched through
Here are the boys' dogs barking at the old woman's dogs

There is the bar where she went each night to sit
There is the sparkling SCHLITZ sign over the mirror
There is the jukebox that only works if you kick it

These are the sleeves she touched each night when she left
These are the dogs coming out of the shadows to join her
These are the ties of the railroad tracks home

Yes
These are the ties of the railroad tracks home.

Glacier

Last night I saw it form again
Along the woods' dark edge;
Heard it gathering out of a wind
From the northwest. Cornflowers
Bent to the earth in its wake,
Animals delved in their burrows,
Leaves stiffened and fell.
I searched through the grass
For a stone scratched by ice,
But could not read its markings
In the faltering light. Found
Another stone smoothed by water,
Opened it to a page of wings.
Lastly an arrowhead. Left
All these things together
In a level field, to be kept
By snow, and raised high or low.

TWO

Mississinewa County Road

WHEN you drive at dusk, alone,
After the corn is harvested, the wind
Scatters bits of dry husk along the road.
A farmer has draped a groundhog's carcass
Across the corner of a wire fence
And the crows have pecked out its eyes.
Your headlights show these things
To a part of your mind that cannot hurry,
That has never learned to decide.
While the car goes on, you get out
And stand with the chaff blowing
And crickets in the grass at the road's edge.
In the distance there is a dog barking
And somewhere a windmill turning in the wind.

The Undertaker

Time came when Sefe Graybill the undertaker—
The only bidder on moving three-hundred-odd graves
From the Mount Moriah churchyard to higher ground
Before the Mississinewa began climbing its banks
To fill the new reservoir—could find no one
In the congregation, none of those helping each other
Move their things out in trucks, who would work for him.

It all had to be dug by hand. Some of the graves
Had been there a hundred years or more. He drove
Through little towns farther north, stopped at taverns
Across from filling stations, at crossroads cafés
Where they still serve a noon plate lunch. Talked
To men who had dug graves, once, with pick and spade,
Back before the war. Machines put them all out of work.

They had found other ways to live. Balding, gray, gone
In the belly, they still needed money. He took them
To the knoll above the covered bridge, paid by the grave.
Each man slowly recognized, like a combination of lost numbers,
That men younger than themselves had labored here,
Grown old, and were gone, who had lifted this same earth,
Who had put in what they now took out, trying not to look

Yet seeing all: that these were the old tools in their hands,
That the sod came up in broken strips, and was cold,
That each shaft found its own way into the darkness,
That even carpenters in those times knew what they built for,
Choosing wood not for the end but the journey, that no jeweler
Had lived among these people, that they had sought remembrance,
That the sun's arc changes with the passage of days.

Sefe could only walk among them, explaining what they saw:
This is a business like any other. Some he had not seen before—
When they brought up what they could find of Amos King
Who had served in the War of 1812, who had helped lay out

The township: an ironstone pipe, a bag of arrowheads,
A Sheffield steel knife. When they brought up his wife:
An ivory medallion of an elephant crushing a man.

Fell overcome with heat, one did, the first day;
Another struck by the sun; two more threw down their tools
And walked away. The few who stayed till the job was done
Rode together in the back of Sefe's pickup each quitting time
To a tavern on the highway, near where they parked.
No one else would go there then. Sat there drinking,
Cursing Sefe, buying him drinks, swearing they could not last.

The Oddfellows' Waiting-Room at Glencove Cemetery

THERE must always be a place like this
Where the dimensions collapse inwardly
Like a telescope you slip into your pocket.
Always a building with gables and arched windows,

Always the polished floorboards of quartersawn oak,
The ceremonial chairs, the lectern, the gavel—
Everything made of oak, and oak outside and alive
Shading this gathering place, measuring light

Falling through glass veins stained green and gold,
Oak nodding with a slow breath of wind in the boughs.
If you could peer downward through this earth
With such clarity, there would be only dust;

If you could peer through the other end of things
There would be only dust too. What light reveals
Here, in this room, is the grain of the bare oak floor
And the shadows of leaves moving with the grain.

Monument City

How I came to that leaf-shadowed house by the river—
   late-summer afternoon rain falling long into evening—
To visit a favorite aunt, who had asked the undertaker—
   his blue pickup truck pulled off just under the willows—

To take photographs of the house, and the gardens,
   and the parlor—with us in it—one last time
Before the waters began to rise, and scavengers came
   to pick over the buildings too big to be moved—

She had seen his truck parked all summer in the churchyard
   on the far side of the covered bridge, with a tent
Pitched first over this headstone, then that, until
   he and his helpers had taken them all up again, like bulbs,

And planted them on higher ground, in a cemetery
   provided by the government. An old friend of his—
This woman with gray braids piled on top of her head,
   who had lived on the corner across from the monument

And taught school thirty-five years until consolidation.
   He still lived on the second floor of the funeral parlor
Down at the crossing, that had been a feedstore once,
   in his father's day. Had carried two wives

Out through those double doors, and a son, to the churchyard.
   He brought with him now a box camera on a wooden tripod
And sat with us there in the parlor till nightfall, waiting
   for the rain to stop, for there to be some light—

How I came to be there that time I cannot remember, only
   walking out to the flowers, at dusk, with the two of them,
Into air fresh from rain, and thunder far away, to the east,
   and lightning that showed us a path through the tall grass.

Roadside Marker

A LIGHT morning snow
Has dusted each letter,
Altering the text:
Now the frontier militia
Cannot find its way
Through the great swamp,
The Indians break camp
And fade into the trees,
There is no dim clearing
Littered with the bodies
Of horses and dying men,
No roadway ahead of you
Scattered with beer cans
And broken glass. Before
You can stop and get out
To touch your fingers
To these words, the sun
Will have turned the page,
The tale will be gilded again.

The Strawman

HANGED for a witch, near a town
In the middle of its own county:
Taken to a field by her neighbors
And ground into the corn stubble.

Who was seen crouched in a room
In an empty house, by three boys
Come for a prank, with flashlights:
Her naked body, caught by the beam,

Entwined with a strawman on the floor.
When the boys told, men went there,
Brought the thing out, showed it
To the women, who knew: creature

Sewn together with bits and pieces
From every dress she made. Dragged her
Forth, then—the seamstress, held
A lantern to her face, saw the eyes

Had no light. Knew this would happen
To her, to them: how each would
Clutch her for a moment, how the strawman
Would rise up in them and dance.

Meditation

THE secret of this countryside
Is in the dream. It is dreamed
Only once, in childhood or old age.
The dreamer is granted the hawk's clarity,
The bee's faceted eye, the omniscience
Of the owl. The land, and all its
Joy and terror and grace
Appear, and appear as a whole:
There are no troubling parts.
The young awake screaming
From this dream, they think
They have seen God, no one
Believes them. The old assume
It is a vision of Death,
Long anticipated, and say nothing.
Both are wrong. It is natural
To speak to Death, even to cry out to him;
Whereas in God's presence
One can only remain silent.

THREE

Work, for the Night Is Coming

On the road out of town past the old quarry
I watched a light rain darkening ledges
Blocked and carded by the drill's bit

Twenty years back. Within those stiff lines,
Places half-stained with damp, the rock face
Opened to a deeper grain—the probable drift

Of the entire ridge outlined for a moment
By the rain's discoloring. Then all turned dim—
Grass holding to the seams, redbud scattered

Across the cliff, dark pool of water
Rimmed with broken stones, where rain, now
Falling steadily, left no lasting pattern.

Bridge over Yellow Cat

WE'D leave before dawn: packed four
To the pickup's front seat, too cold
To ride in back, somebody'd be sitting
On somebody else's knees. Shorty'd stop
Every ten or fifteen miles to get out
And lash the walers down again,
Make sure the red flannel flag
Hadn't blown away. That old truck
Didn't have any radio, only one
Windshield wiper that worked. We'd talk
About things you could see from the road,
And things you couldn't see,
That were gone now: glazed-brick silo
Where you turned off for the sawmill;
Boarded-up truckstop, pumps rusted,
"All the fried chicken you can eat";
Chinquapin oak the doctor's son hit
Head-on coming home from the prom.
There's fog in early mornings, even
In summer: low patches that rise like dust
From a fresh stone road. My father talked
About people he had known—masons,
Carpenters, finishers, old-timers who
Carried their tools in canvas satchels,
Never took their shirts off in the sun.
Dead, now, most of them; or drunk.
Sometimes we didn't say anything,
Just sat there—the four of us,
Driving into the red morning light
To build a bridge over Yellow Cat.

Watching by the Stream

You've already noticed that in this town
They don't put the walleyed people away.
They let them wander around, like moths
That cannot find the way to light.
The concrete parkbench bolted to the bank
Fills up late Saturday afternoons
With parts of three-piece pin-striped suits
And coats worn through at the elbows
And shiny gabardine pants—thrown out
Each spring by others in the town. Others
Who now no longer recognize themselves
In these mashed, crooked faces.
The old men talk among themselves:
About the price of ginseng,
And the 32-pound albino coon
Slick Baxter's redbones finally treed,
And the ring around the moon last night.
You already know all that. Because
In the long evenings you have stood there
Listening, watching their walleyes stray
About your shoulders. They know who you are.
They peer into you sideways
Like a doctor looking underneath a bandage.
They used to play ice hockey on the creek
With your grandfather, who lived out by Hobbs;
They helped build a bridge once with your father;
They even knew your Aunt Tiz, before she left.
They gaze into that thicket now with their walleyes.
One eye stays on you, the other searches
As though feeling in the dark
Along a partially familiar earthen wall.
You have already stood there watching them
Watch you. They tell their stories anyway.
This is what you have come to hear.
Tonight they are talking about cripples
And how they got that way. Remember

[25]

Lester Crabtree, the one-armed drayman,
Who used to waltz with the old upright
In the ballroom over the Eagles' Lodge?
Lost his in a train wreck, six people dead,
Up near Lafayette, on the Monon line. And
Abe Branitsky, who sold crackers and sausage
To the boys down at the mill. Abe lost his arm
In the Kaiser's war. And when the engineer
Who came to tell them how to take the mill down
Walked in his store to buy a dope, Abe shot him
Right between the eyes, and got off clean
In self-defense. And tell of Brian DeWeese
Whose father traveled all the way from Wales
To show them how to work the tin, Brian
Who mangled both his hands in the roller-house
And whimpered like a dog when old Doc Burns
Had to cut them off the rest of the way.
And how before the stumps were healed he walked
To Middletown, and paid a harness-maker
To build a frame of ash and leather strips
That held a Smith and Wesson .44.
He learned to fire it with a piece of twine
Held in his teeth, practiced in an orchard,
Blasting at green apples, steadying
His aim, working the contraption before him
Like some thick brown insect that had landed
On his arms, and was eating him away.
And Doc in his office drinking grain alcohol,
Playing pinochle with his driver, Eddie McMinn.
When Brian comes to town to find the doc
Nobody goes outside, you can hear pigeons
Cooing in the First Methodist Church belfry.
Doc finally comes out, Brian readies
The apparatus, sights down the barrel, fires.
Doc climbs into his buggy and drives away.
Brian DeWeese hauled trash till the day he died.

They can see him now, every man on the bench,
Their walleyes swinging into focus—
Eyes that have seen grace in a thousand jump shots
And the beauty of waitresses in all-night truckstops
And rain coming down the window beneath the neon sign—
Eyes that see Brian DeWeese dropping away
From the dump truck's runningboard
And bursting with both thick iron hooks
Into a fifty-gallon drum of garbage,
Emptying it over his head into the truck
Like a bear shaking a log full of ants.
You look, at that moment, into the stream
That they keep watch by, these old men
Who used to know Max Quick, before the fire,
And wrestled with Pegleg McGee for fifty cents.
Their walleyes drift like white fish in a cave.
They watch the air about you as though light
Were coming through the depths of your blood.

At the Sign-Painter's

Of them all—those laboring men who knew my first name
And called out to me as I watched them coming up the walk;
The ones with birthmarks and missing fingers and red hair,
Who had worked for my grandfather, and now my father;
Who had gone home to wash up and put on a clean shirt;
Who came to the back door Friday evenings for their checks;
Who drove a Ford coupe and had a second wife and three kids
And were headed for town to have a drink and buy groceries—

Of the ones too old to work—in their black shoes laced up
With hooks, and their string ties, who stood on the sidewalk
Where we were building something, and asked my father
If he remembered the house-moving business back during
The Depression: how you squirmed through all that dust
And broken glass in the crawl space, nudging ten-by-twelves
Twenty feet long, and lugged the house-jacks behind you
One at a time, setting them up just right. How you moved
On your back like a crab through darkness, cobwebs
Brushing your face, an iron bar in your hands, a voice
Calling somewhere from outside, asking for a quarter-turn—

Of them all—plumbers, tinners, roofers, well-diggers,
Carpenters, cement finishers with their padded knees—
I liked the sign-painters best: liked being taken there
By my father, following after him, running my fingers
Along the pipe railing, taking his hand as we climbed up
The concrete embankment to their back-street shop looking
Out across the Nickel Plate yard—
                                    liked being left to wander
Among piles of fresh pine planks, tables caked and smeared
And stacked with hundreds of bottles and jars leaking color
And fragrance, coffee cans jammed with dried brushes, skylight
Peppered with dead flies, narrow paths that wound among
Signs shrouded with tape and newspaper—all the way back
To the airshaft, the blackened sink, the two-burner hotplate,
Spoons sticking from china mugs, behind the curtain the bed

With its torn army blanket—liked feeling beneath my toes
The wood floors patterned with forgotten colors, soft
To the step, darkened with grime and soot from the trains—

Liked them most of all—those solemn old men with skin
Bleached and faded as their hair, white muslin caps
Speckled with paint, knuckles and fingers faintly dotted—
Liked them for their listening to him about the sign
He wanted painted, for pretending not to notice me watching—
For the wooden rod with its black knob resting lightly
Against the primed surface, for the slow sweep and whisper
Of the brush—liked seeing the ghost letters in pencil
Gradually filling out, fresh and wet and gleaming, words
Forming out of all that darkness, that huge disorder.

Turning the Brick

MEN worked turning the brick
At the end of our street—
They gave each one a quarter-turn
And put it back again. That

Was what the Depression was like
Where I grew up. Each day
They got closer to our house;
Everybody came out to watch.

They had their shirts off,
Down on their knees—old scars
Flared in the sunlight, tattoos
Glistened on their arms. Men

With no teeth, with noses
Turned and bent, fingers missing.
The bricks were tan-colored;
Each had a picture on the bottom:

A scene of ships, a name, a date.
One of the men brushed the sand
From a brick and held it out.
We gathered around. He let us touch

The rough emblem, the letters,
The year. He gave the brick
A quarter-turn, put it back
In the street, and went on.

FOUR

Tintypes

1

Sam Bass

Train robber and outlaw, born near Mitchell,
Indiana, 1851, died Round Rock, Texas, 1878.

THEY did not quarry limestone in those days.
They sat around the general store, and spit,
Or killed animals for their pelts
Or grubbed in the dirt each spring.
I loved horses, always horses,
It was a horse that got me away from there,
A horse that took me to Texas,
A horse that made me somebody: the Denton mare.
She could outrun any horse alive—
And any mail train, too. It was a horse,
Finally, that carried me out of Round Rock
After the ambush, when three of us
Stood off thirty of them, when Barnes
Took a bullet in the head, and a Ranger
Shot me in the back. We got away,
And Jackson wanted me to lie in the creek
So the mud would take out the poison.
I couldn't ride. I gave him my pistol
And my last double eagle. He tethered
The horse, and I waited under a tree
All night for the posse to find me.
It took three days for me to bleed to death.
People crowded around the shack
Where they had me, but I never talked.
If a man knows anything
He ought to die with it in him.

Oliver P. Morton

Governor of Indiana during Civil War.
Born Wayne County, Indiana, 1823, died
Washington, D.C., 1877.

I was being shaved by old Jake Dunn
The morning the news came:
Morgan and 2,500 men and horses
Across the Ohio, heading north. I decided
To have Jake give me a haircut, too.
Think of war. Think of armies marching,
Of chimneys belching the smoke
Of iron and munitions, of rails,
Of cannon and ships, of Old Glory
Snapping above the columns of blue.
Why, in a matter of hours
I mobilized 30,000 old men and boys
To go chasing around after Morgan;
Who was, of course, a joke.
Telegrams outrun horses any day.
There are callow historians
Who spend lifetimes in dim libraries
Writing about that silly raid.
Let them. Morgans come and go.
No matter how appropriate some might deem it
My monument is not an iron statue
For pigeons to spatter on the statehouse lawn.
No, it is my spirit that endures.
A century later, how many Hoosiers give a damn
If black men and women are oppressed?
But in a matter of hours you can scare up
Any number of men and boys in this state
To go out and try to kill somebody.

John Dillinger

Bank robber and desperado, born Indianapolis,
1902, died Chicago, 1934.

MORE than mobility,
More than communications,
Even more than guts: imagination.
I stick in your craw, O Hoosier Commonwealth,
Because I made it look easy.
I cleaned out your tinhorn banks and arsenals,
I bamboozled your redneck sheriffs and jailers—
And yawned. You would like to believe
That I was Robin Hood,
That I fooled the city slickers too.
But your editors insist—
Because they are hired to insist—
That I was a no-good rotten punk.
In fact, I was the original
"Public Enemy Number One."
Hoover invented me. The Bureau invented itself
In the process of saving you from me.
Remember that, the next time the
Smooth-talking agent in the drip-
Dry suit knocks on your door
To ask you a few questions.
Beware those who grow fat and sleek
Imagining enemies.

FIVE

Landing the Bees

for George P. Elliott

First the bough of the apple bending; neighbors
Calling to one another in their watery voices,
None venturing close to the glittering branch.

They make way for the old bee-man, in his felt hat,
Who spreads a sheet on the grass, a white sheet
From his own bed; and with a pocket mirror

Casts the sun's image up into the swarm.
If you have walked in sleep, you know this movement
Out through air, through blossoming, down

To a new place, drawn by a brilliance in the leaves
And folded into whiteness. He takes them up
As though carrying coals. If you have wakened

Arms outstretched, you know this moment: things
Rising of their own accord are beckoning
To themselves. It is your own voice murmuring.

The Measuring

You're sickly pale—a crooked root.
But one last remedy remains:
Before the dawn we'll go on foot
Through grass sleeked down by heavy rains
To the sexton's house. Already he
Takes down his spade, and goes
To walk among the whitened rows.
His wife awaits with lengths of string
Necessary for measuring.

She has no fire alight, nor words
To spare, but bolts the wooden door
And helps you out of clothes that fall
Soundlessly to the floor. Naked,
You mount the table and recline;
She comes, her eight stiff fingers
Trailing bright bits of twine. First
Crown to nose, then mouth to chin,
Pressing against each crevice, in
And down the length of your cold frame—
Whispering unintelligible names.

The feet are last to stretch: from heel
To toe each one must be times seven
The other piece. She nods, and knots
The two together, breathes her spell,
Then turns to go. I leave a pair
Of silver dollars there, and take
The string to tie where it will rot
The winter long: on hinge of gate,
Wheelbarrow shaft, or eaves-trough's fall.

Behind us, where the darkness drains,
A blackbird settles on the roof
And calls back to another that rain
Is coming like an awful proof.

The two denounce the scratching sound
The sexton's spade makes on the ground—
Measuring off the careful square
Of someone else expected there.

Gathering Fireflies

for Selene

It is of days lost, and found, this old ritual
Of midsummer twilight. She has heard me tell
Of that stilled, silken procession
Passing among the stone walls of the village
And into the forest, the evening a basket
Of candles swinging to the river's pulse.

So we take an empty mayonnaise jar
To the sidewalk, and tools from the shed
(Ten-penny nail and wooden-handled hammer),
And drive a tinny star of holes into the lid.
Everything must breathe, even the leaves
That light up now with cold beckoning.

Always I have been reluctant to sleep
In summer evenings, when dusk has the texture
Of linen spread out over long grass. She has
My green eyes, my slender fingers, my dread
Of this time; and now will exorcise
The darkening, gathering her quick lantern.

Whether I could still find it, the path
To the bonfire; whether I could locate
Among constellations the unturning point—
All this fades in her dance of evening,
Fades and comes to pass again, familiar
And strange as the glass she brandishes.

Ginseng

A GOD-FEARING man did not labor
On the Sabbath, or witch for water
During the week, or work charms
For warts or rain. When he told her
We were going to the bottomland
After Sunday dinner, it would be
To see if that oak limb had fallen yet
Or whether the crows were in the corn.
The scythe would be hidden already
Out by the gate, buried knee-deep
In Queen Anne's lace. We would sit
On the front-porch swing listening
To her read scripture, until bees
Drifting about the clematis vine
Made her drowsy. When she leaned
Into sleep, he eased her body
Against the cushions, and waved me
Toward the gate.

           I think we became
Her dream: child with the same eyes
And silver hair as his, running bare-
Headed; old man bent like the scythe
He carried—for no apparent reason,
No grass high enough there to mow,
The land swept clean by the glacier,
By ten thousand years of the creek
Switching its tail back and forth;
And at least twenty head of cattle
Grazing the last hundred.

            Beyond
The pasture they had railed off
A branch of the creek for thistles
And jimsonweed. We walked there,

The scythe in my hands now, since
Those who taught him had carried one
When looking for ginseng: something
To have with you at the first place
You come to, so that you may nod,
And pass by; something to lean on
When you find the right cluster
And stand looking down at it—
Wondering how many dry-weight ounces
Of root it would yield, how long
It has been growing there, who else
Had harvested it since the Nanticoke
Passed through here gathering things
Before there were roads.

               Even now,
He explained, men dig it up, ruin
Whole stands, steal it from farmers.
But all of them together—hunters,
Thieves, those who keep the old ways—
Pass it from hand to hand along
A chain of those who know exactly
Where it is going, what it is worth—
Until eventually it arrives
On the other side of the world,
Where it is ground into dust
And mixed into potions they say
Can make an old man young again.

Going back, he would let me carry
The scythe, to leave it hidden
Once more in the weeds by the gate.
She would be up and waiting for us
By the well, and I would pump
While they splashed water on their faces.

When she awoke with the Book in her lap,
She said, and looked at the two of us
Coming across the ridge in the heat,
We seemed to shimmer, to step toward her
Like two unexpected messengers
Come from an old story. For a moment
She could even make out the cord
That bound us together—now long,
Like an arm stretched between us,
Now like a vein of lightning opening.

Shaking the Peonies

for Effie

I WOULD lie down again in your bed of fabrications
Like a quilt of many voices covering me in darkness—
Colors stitched from the motions of your hands bringing water
From low places, or your kneeling each morning to build a fire
As though the sun had come to call, and we were all new.

I would sit peeling apples with you in the plum-tree shade,
Waiting for the four-o'clocks to open. When the dog
Found his corner at bedtime, I would again watch his turning,
Hear your voice, and see immemorial grasses bending.
When you asked, the longlegs pointed the way of the wind;
When you put the shell to my ear, I heard the sea.

I would go again with you carrying cans of bright flowers,
Heavy iron shears, sun hats made of straw, and gloves—
Peonies falling over drowsy to the ground by that day
And gathered in bunches ivory and white like girls
Gowned in green leaves. I would imitate your swinging
As you show me how to shake off the ants, and they fall.

Go following after you on that day of light and stones
Lodged in a green meadow: to place the blades of grass again
In order; to trace the hard insignia of hearts, smooth links'
Of chain, and tools; to be again there with you encountering
Old friends, who also come to decorate each year, who speak
Of times when you were young together. Listening to voices

Admiring the flame of blossoms, the bees, the white lamb
That waits on the stone: would hear pollen in these shadows—
All the naming, gathering of things, parts innumerable
That make up this world. There I would lie down again, yes
And become whole, like the ending of a story, and sleep.

The Birdstone

for Cameron Parks

Of the traditional priestly tasks,
The offices carried out by the elders,
The secrets entrusted: the birdstone
Bears these in its beak like a slate feather.

No one touches this feather, it is a song
My grandfather taught me for twirling
The fire-bow, for hewing the ax-head,
For weaving the platform of nettles.

When the last breath goes out of a man
He must wait above the earth in the sun
And the rain until the old songs leave him
Like smoke, like a plume blown by the wind.

When I die finally and you bind it
Against my wrinkled forehead
The birdstone will confirm all this for you
And brush your lips, once, with its stiff wings.

ABOUT THE AUTHOR

Jared Carter was born in Elwood, Indiana, in 1939, and now lives in Indianapolis. He attended Yale University and Goddard College and has worked as a reporter, textbook editor, and book designer. Mr. Carter is a founding editor of *Indiana Arts Insight* and contributing editor to *Indiana Writes*. His poetry has appeared in *The Nation*, *Prairie Schooner*, and *College English*, as well as other publications and anthologies. In 1979, a chapbook of his work entitled *Early Warning* was published by the Barnwood Press Cooperative. He is co-author, with Richard Balkin, of *A Writer's Guide to Book Publishing*.